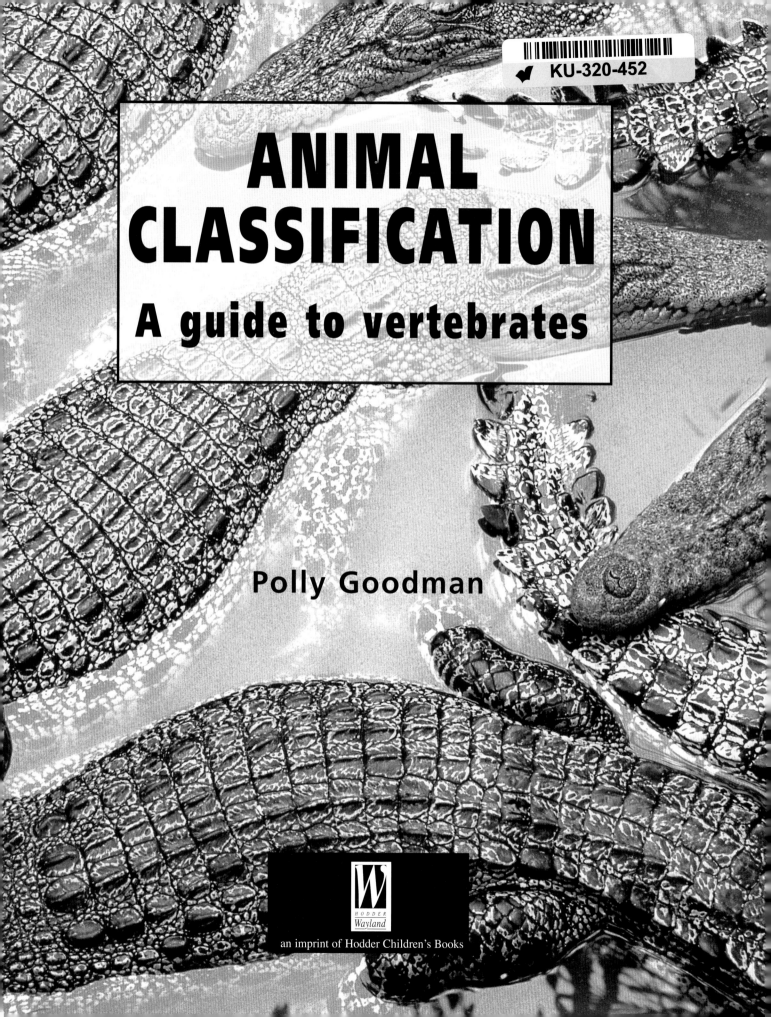

ANIMAL CLASSIFICATION

A guide to vertebrates

Polly Goodman

HODDER
Wayland

an imprint of Hodder Children's Books

Also in the series: Plant Classification

Animal Classification is an updated version of Hodder Wayland's Classification: The Animal Kingdom

Text copyright © Hodder Wayland 2004
Volume copyright © Hodder Wayland 2004

Editor: Katie Sergeant
Designer: Simon Borrough
Typesetter: Jane Hawkins
Cover design: Hodder Children's Books

First published in 1999 by Wayland Publishers Ltd.
This edition updated and published in 2004 by
Hodder Wayland, an imprint of Hodder Children's
Books

British Library Cataloguing in Publication Data
  Goodman, Polly
  1. Zoology - Classification - Juvenile literature
  2. Animal diversity - Juvenile literature
  I. Title
  590.1'2

ISBN 0750245832

Printed and bound in China

Hodder Children's Books
A division of Hodder Headline Limited
338 Euston Road, London NW1 3BH

Cover: The Toco toucan (*Ramphastos toco*) is the biggest member of the toucan family. It uses its large beak to skin fruit, drill wood looking for insects, or tear the flesh of young birds.

Title page: An overhead view of crocodiles, crowded together in a pool.

Below: Blue tits feed their young on caterpillars. Feeding is busiest in the mornings, when the adult may make up to 72 trips to the nest each hour.

CONTENTS

THE KINGDOMS

There are over 2 million types of living things in the world. To help study them and avoid confusion, scientists have sorted, or 'classified', them into groups according to their similarities and differences. New discoveries are being made all the time and added to the classification system.

Most scientists divide the entire living world into five groups, called kingdoms. These kingdoms are: animals, plants, fungi, protists and monerans. Each kingdom is divided into smaller and smaller groups, each of which have more and more features in common.

The smallest groups are called species. They contain living things that share two main characteristics: first, they look similar; and second, members of the same species can breed together in the wild.

▲ The elephant is the largest land animal in the world. This is the African elephant, or *Loxodonta africana.*

Names

Most living things have a common name, such as 'beetle' or 'cat'. But there are about 300,000 species of beetles in the world, and 37 species of cats. Also, common names change in different languages. To help identify each species more accurately, in the eighteenth century, a Swedish scientist called Carolus Linnaeus (1707–78) gave them Latin names as well. Each species' Latin name is the same all over the world.

This book looks at part of the animal kingdom. It looks at vertebrates, which all have backbones. Vertebrates are divided into five classes of animals: fish, amphibians, reptiles, birds, and mammals.

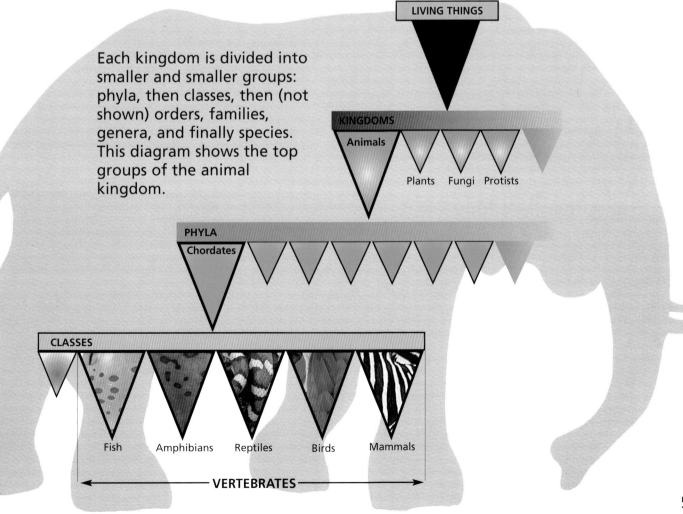

Each kingdom is divided into smaller and smaller groups: phyla, then classes, then (not shown) orders, families, genera, and finally species. This diagram shows the top groups of the animal kingdom.

LIVING THINGS

KINGDOMS
Animals   Plants   Fungi   Protists

PHYLA
Chordates

CLASSES
Fish   Amphibians   Reptiles   Birds   Mammals

← VERTEBRATES →

FISH

Fish first appeared in the oceans almost 500 million years ago. Today there are about 30,000 species living in the world's rivers, lakes and oceans. Fish have adapted well to living in the water. They breathe mainly with gills, which absorb oxygen from the water. Most fish have fins and are streamlined to help them move through the water.

▲The whale shark (*Rhincodon typus*) is the largest shark in the world.

Characteristics of fish
- breathe with gills
- have scaly skin
- live in water
- have fins and/or tails for swimming

Habitat

Fish live almost anywhere there is water, which covers about three-quarters of the Earth's surface. Most species live in the oceans. Only about 2,500 species live in rivers and lakes. Almost all fish are cold-blooded, which means their body temperature is about the same as the water around them.

Groups

Fish can be divided into three main groups: bony fish, cartilaginous fish and jawless fish. Over 95 per cent of fish are bony fish, which contains about 24,000 species.

Goldfish, cod and trout are all bony fish. All bony fish have skeletons that are made of bone. Most species have a gas-filled bag called a swim bladder, which holds the fish up in the water.

Cartilaginous fish, such as sharks, skates and rays, have skeletons made of cartilage. They have no swim bladder, so to keep afloat, they have to keep swimming using their powerful tails and fins. Jawless fish make up only 1 per cent of fish species. Instead of jaws, they have round, sucking mouths.

◄ The blue spotted stingray (*Taeniura lymma*) is a cartilaginous fish. It does not need a streamlined body because it spends most of its time on the ocean floor.

Senses

All fish can detect movements in the water using their lateral line. This is a series of sensitive pores that runs down the sides of their bodies. It can sense movements in the water caused by currents, predators, prey and other fish.

Most fish can hear well, even though they have no external ear. They also have a good sense of smell, which helps to detect food and predators. Fish use taste buds in their mouth, and often on their lips, fins and other parts of their body, to recognise food and avoid poisonous substances.

Many species of catfish have taste buds on whisker-like projections called barbels, which help find food on the riverbed. ▶

Sharks, rays and other cartilaginous fish can only see in black and white, but many bony fish can see in colour. Four-eyed fish, which live on the surface of the water, have eyes divided into two halves. They can see above the water and below it at the same time.

Colour

Most fish are coloured to match their surroundings, which helps hide them from predators. Some have eyespots on their bodies to confuse predators. Many bony fish are brightly coloured, especially those living in coral reefs. Their colours blend in with their surroundings and help to attract mates.

The archer fish (*Toxotes chatereus*) shoots down prey living above the water using a jet of water forced out of its mouth.

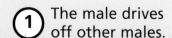 The male drives off other males.

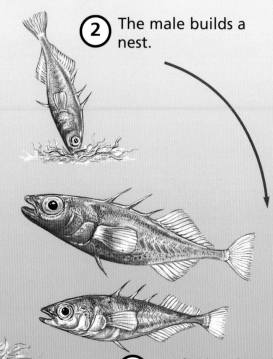 The male builds a nest.

Breeding

Most bony fish lay eggs. The female lays a large number of eggs in the water, which are fertilised by the male's sperm. Only a few of the eggs will survive to become adults. Some cartilaginous fish and bony fish do not lay eggs. They produce live young.

He finds a female stickleback.

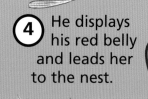 He displays his red belly and leads her to the nest.

Courtship

Many fish have dramatic courtship rituals. This page shows the courtship of the stickleback. In the mating season, in the spring or summer, the male stickleback's belly turns red to attract females. First, the male drives other males from his territory and builds a nest. Then he attracts a female and leads her to his nest. The female lays her eggs in the nest, which the male fertilises and then guards from predators.

The female lays her eggs in the nest.

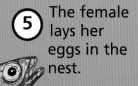

The male fertilises the eggs.

The male protects the fry (young) when they hatch.

10

Salmon are powerful swimmers and can leap out of the water to cross waterfalls. Brown bears stand in wait and try to catch them as they leap.

Migration of fish

Some species of fish travel long distances to lay their eggs. Salmon spend most of their lives in the ocean, but they migrate up rivers to breed and lay their eggs. The eggs hatch on riverbeds. When they are two or three years old, the young salmon start the long journey to the sea. If they survive, the salmon stay at sea for one to four years, before returning to the river of their birth to lay eggs.

AMPHIBIANS

Amphibians evolved from fish about 350 million years ago.

The word 'amphibian' comes from the Greek words meaning 'double life', because many amphibians have two stages of life. The young larvae, or tadpoles, live in water. The adults live on land. The tadpoles become adults through a process called metamorphosis.

▲ Caecilians are legless, worm-like amphibians. They live in underground burrows in tropical parts of the world.

Characteristics of amphibians
• have smooth, moist skin
• live in damp places
• adults breathe through their skins as well as with lungs

Amphibians can be divided into three groups: frogs and toads, newts and salamanders, and caecilians. The biggest group is frogs and toads, which has about 4,000 different species.

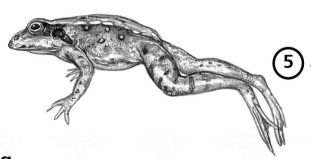

(5) Adult frog.

Breeding

Amphibians live in moist habitats, near ponds, lakes, or streams. Most amphibians mate and lay their eggs in water. The eggs are covered in a clear jelly, called spawn. The eggs hatch into larvae, or tadpoles. The tadpoles use gills to breathe underwater, and move using fins and a tail.

As they metamorphose (change) into adults, most tadpoles lose their tail and grow legs to walk and jump. They lose their gills and grow lungs to breathe. Adult amphibians breathe through their skin as well as with lungs. Their skin has to be soft and damp to be able to breathe, which is why amphibians have to live close to water.

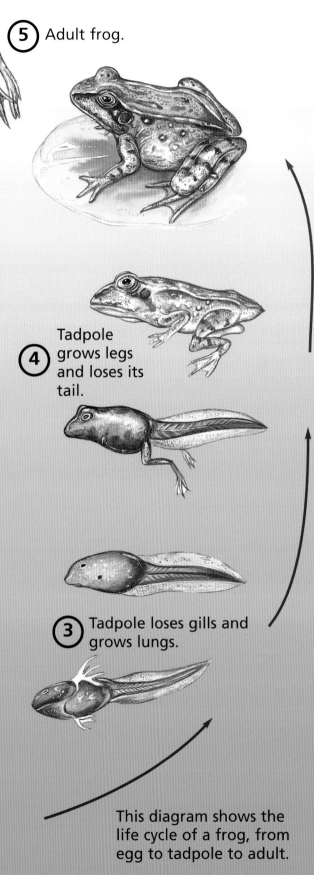

(4) Tadpole grows legs and loses its tail.

(3) Tadpole loses gills and grows lungs.

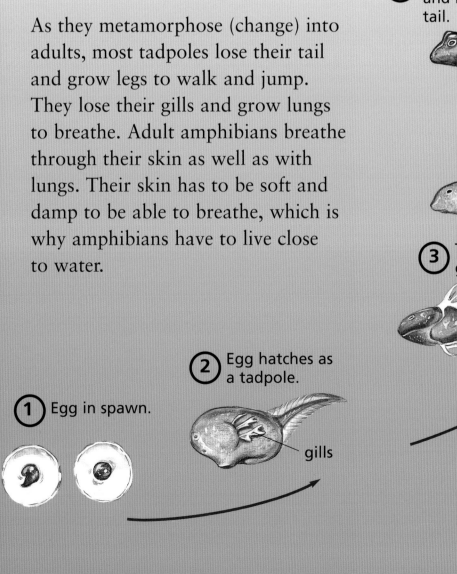

(2) Egg hatches as a tadpole.

(1) Egg in spawn.

gills

This diagram shows the life cycle of a frog, from egg to tadpole to adult.

Self-defence

Amphibians have many predators, including lizards and mammals. They have various ways of avoiding them. Frogs and toads can escape predators by leaping away using their long back legs. Some salamanders can shed their tails if they are attacked.

Many amphibians have skin colours that camouflage them against their surroundings, to help hide from predators. Others ooze poison from a special gland and are brightly coloured to warn predators.

The fire-bellied toad (*Bombina orientalis*) has a bright-red belly to warn predators that it is poisonous. ▶

Feeding

Most amphibians eat insects. Many, including frogs, toads and salamanders, catch their prey using their long, sticky tongue. They swallow their food whole, blinking as they swallow to make their eyeballs push downwards and squeeze food down their throat.

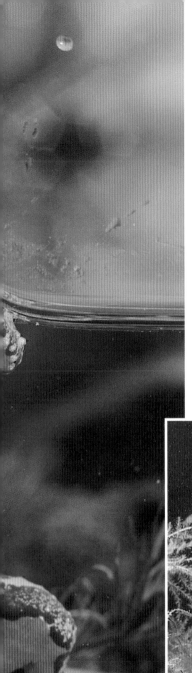

Senses

Most amphibians have a good sense of touch. Those living in water sense movement in the same way as fish, using their lateral line system (see page 8). Most frogs, toads and salamanders have good eyesight, whereas many caecilians, who live in underground burrows, are blind.

Frogs and toads have loud calls and better hearing than caecilians and salamanders. Caecilians and most salamanders have no voice.

▲ Some amphibians, such as this axolotl (*Ambystoma mexicanum*), stay in their tadpole form all their lives.

REPTILES

Reptiles evolved from amphibians about 300 million years ago. There are about 6,500 species alive today, most of which live on land.

The gecko (*Gecko gecko*) is a type of lizard. It can walk up walls and upside-down across ceilings. ▶

Characteristics of reptiles
- have dry, scaly, waterproof skin
- breathe with lungs
- live on land in warm habitats
- lay eggs with shells
- fully formed young hatch from shells

▲ A mountain king snake (*Lampropeltis pyromelana*) basks in the sun of the Arizona desert, USA.

Keeping warm

Reptiles can be divided into four groups: lizards and snakes, tortoises and turtles, crocodilians, and the tuatara. Like fish and amphibians, reptiles are cold-blooded, which means their body temperature is similar to their surroundings. Since they rely on the sun's heat to warm their blood, most reptiles are found in warm regions of the world. These include swamps, rivers, rainforests and deserts.

Reptiles use different methods to control their body temperature. To warm their blood they bask in the sun. To cool down, crocodiles rest with their mouths open, allowing heat to escape. Other reptiles move under shade or into water to cool down.

◄ Cobras have fangs at the front of their mouth.

Vipers and adders have fangs that fold back against the roof of the mouth when not in use. ►

Snakes

Snakes are thought to have developed from lizards that burrowed underground. Their lack of legs and streamlined shape would have helped them move through the soil. Today there are about 2,700 species, most of which live above ground. Some move by wriggling from side to side. Others move forwards by repeatedly bunching up and straightening.

Snakes feed on birds, mammals, frogs and reptiles. Some snakes kill their prey by squeezing them to death. These are known as constrictors. Others kill using poison, which they inject into their prey through their fangs. These are called venomous snakes.

▲ Some snakes have fangs at the back of the mouth.

Lizards

There are almost 4,000 species of lizards. Lizards have four legs and eyelids that move. Many have specially adapted feet and toes for getting around. Climbing lizards, such as geckos, have pads on their toes that cling to smooth surfaces, allowing them to walk across ceilings.

Most lizards are well camouflaged and hide from predators. Others surprise enemies by suddenly expanding the skin around their neck, which confuses the enemy and gives them time to escape. Many lizards shed their tail when under attack. They will grow another one later.

Tuatara

The tuatara is only found on the small islands off New Zealand. It is the only surviving member of a group of reptiles that lived over 200 million years ago, at the time of the dinosaurs.

Unlike other lizards, chameleons have tails that can grasp objects, such as the branches of trees in which they live. ▼

Crocodilians

Crocodiles, alligators and caimans belong to the group of reptiles called crocodilians. They lurk in tropical swamps, rivers and lakes.

Adult crocodilians are fierce hunters, attacking fish and mammals the size of antelopes. They ambush prey and drag it underwater until it drowns. Since crocodilians cannot chew, they tear apart their food by shaking it.

The biggest group is the crocodiles. Female crocodiles lay their eggs in nests of vegetation or bury them in holes. The females of some species guard the eggs until they are hatched and carry them to the water in their mouths.

The American alligator (*Alligator mississipiensis*) grows to about 4 metres long.

▲ These female olive ridley turtles (*Lepidochelys olivacea*) are digging holes on a beach for their eggs.

Tortoises and turtles

There are over 250 species of tortoises, turtles and terrapins, all of which have a hard shell. Most tortoises and turtles can pull their head, legs and tail back inside their shell, making it impossible for predators to get at them. The shells also provide camouflage.

Most tortoises live on land, while turtles live in the sea. Tortoises have strong, thick legs to support their weight on land, while turtles have wing-shaped flippers for legs which are ideal for swimming.

Female tortoises and turtles lay their eggs in holes in the ground. They cover them with soil or sand and leave them to incubate under the heat of the sun. When the young hatch, they have to dig their way to the surface.

BIRDS

Birds evolved from reptiles about 140 million years ago. There are about 9,600 species known today, from the smallest hummingbird to the largest ostrich.

All birds have wings and feathers, and most can fly. Not all birds fly, however. Ostriches run instead of flying and penguins swim.

Birds are well adapted for flying. They have a light skeleton where many of the larger bones are hollow. Powerful flight muscles are attached to the skeleton. Their feathers are made of keratin, which is the same lightweight substance as nails and hair. Birds use their feathers to fly and also to keep warm.

Characteristics of birds
- have feathers
- breathe with lungs
- warm-blooded
- have a hard bill or beak
- lay eggs with shells
- incubate eggs with their bodies

The African ostrich (*Struthio camelus*) is the world's largest bird. It cannot fly but can run up to 70 kph. ▶

Wing shapes

The shape of a bird's wings affects how fast it can fly:

The albatross has long slender ▶ wings for gliding above the oceans.

The buzzard soars on its broad wings while looking for prey. ▶

The swallow has pointed wings for flying fast and catching insects. ▶

Jays have rounded wings for twisting through trees as they look for nuts. ▶

◀ Sparrows and other small birds have wings that let them fly quickly over short distances.

◀ Hummingbirds have narrow wings that beat 50–80 times a minute as they hover above flowers feeding on nectar.

A barn owl (*Tyto alba*) uses its feathers as a brake as it comes to rest. ▼

Feathers

Birds regularly look after their feathers by straightening them and removing parasites. This is called preening. They use their bill to comb the feathers and put them back into place. Most birds also cover their feathers with oil, produced from a gland near the base of the tail. The oil keeps the feathers supple and waterproof.

Food

Birds are warm-blooded. They control their body temperature by burning food. They also eat food to give them energy for flying. Smaller birds, such as swallows and sparrows, mainly eat insects, seeds, fruits and nectar. Larger birds of prey, such as eagles and falcons, eat fish and small mammals.

Birds gather and bite food using their beak, or bill. The shape of a bird's beak depends on its diet. Birds of prey have a hooked bill for tearing flesh, while hummingbirds have long, slender bills for sucking nectar from flowers.

The shape of birds' feet also varies, depending on how they live.

◀ Parrots eat nuts and seeds. They hold food in their feet and crack it open using their strong, hooked beak.

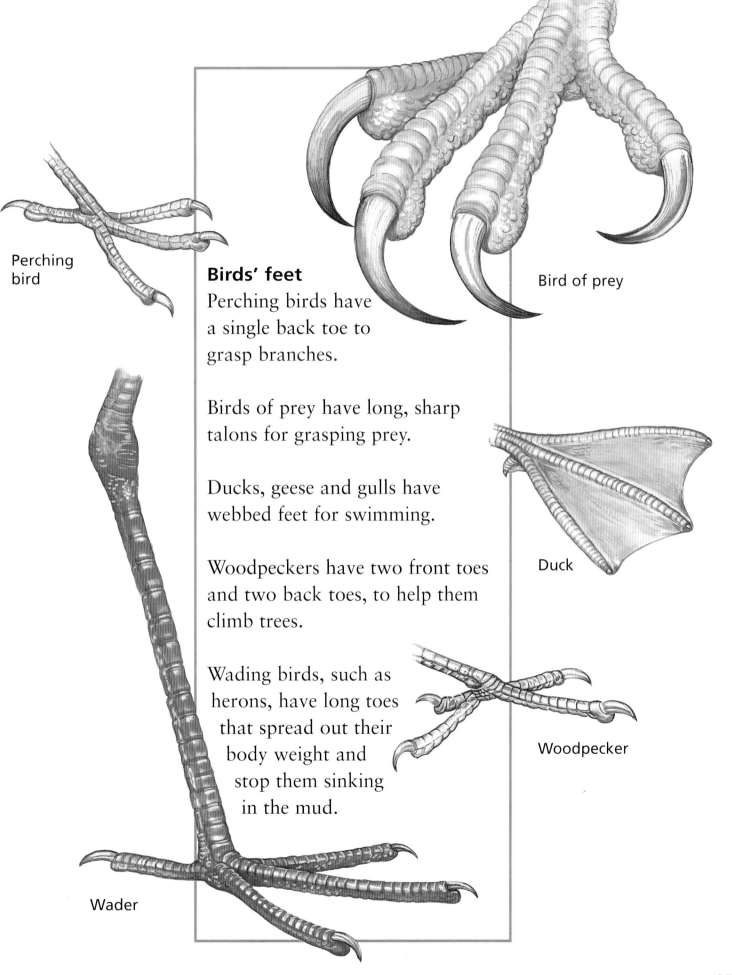

Perching bird

Bird of prey

Duck

Woodpecker

Wader

Birds' feet

Perching birds have
a single back toe to
grasp branches.

Birds of prey have long, sharp
talons for grasping prey.

Ducks, geese and gulls have
webbed feet for swimming.

Woodpeckers have two front toes
and two back toes, to help them
climb trees.

Wading birds, such as
herons, have long toes
that spread out their
body weight and
stop them sinking
in the mud.

The male Cape weaver (*Ploceus capensis*) hangs from his nest of grasses to attract a female.

Breeding

Birds mate in the spring. At that time, male birds find a territory and attract a female in a courtship display. Before the eggs are laid, most female birds build a nest out of mud, twigs and leaves. Some birds do not build nests but use hollow trees or other birds' nests instead. Others lay their eggs in holes or vegetation on the ground.

Incubation

Most female birds incubate their eggs by sitting on them to keep them warm while the embryos grow inside. The male often helps the female by bringing her food. However, some birds do not incubate their eggs. Some cuckoos lay their eggs in another bird's nest and leave them to be incubated by the other bird.

Senses

Birds have very good senses of sight and hearing. However, they have poor senses of smell, taste and touch. Birds of prey have eyes that face forwards, which help them judge distance when swooping down on prey. Other birds have eyes on the sides of their head, which are good for spotting predators.

◀ A male bird of paradise (*Paradisaea rubra*) shows off his colourful feathers in a courtship display.

MAMMALS

Mammals evolved from reptiles about 220 million years ago. The first mammals were probably small, shrew-like creatures. There are over 4,000 species of mammals today that have adapted to all the world's habitats.

All mammals are warm-blooded, which means they control their body temperature by burning food. Unlike reptiles, amphibians and birds, all mammals feed their young on milk. They use lungs to breathe and most have hairy, smooth, dry skin.

The duck-billed platypus (*Ornithorhynchus anatinus*) is a mammal because it feeds its young on milk. ▼

Characteristics of mammals
- have fur or hair
- breathe with lungs
- feed their young on milk
- are warm-blooded

Groups

Mammals can be divided into three main groups: monotremes, marsupials and placental mammals. Each group differs in the way it raises its young.

Monotremes, which include the platypus and the spiny anteater, are the only mammals to lay eggs. When the eggs hatch, the young feed on milk from their mother.

Marsupials, such as the kangaroo and koala, mostly live in Australasia. They give birth to young that are not fully formed. The young complete their growth for up to 11 months in a pouch on their mother's belly.

▲ This killer whale calf (*Orcinus orca*) is taking milk from its mother.

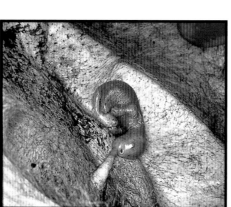

◀ This blind, newborn kangaroo is feeding on one of its mother's teats in her pouch.

Most mammals are placental mammals. The young in this group complete their growth inside their mother's body, where they are protected and receive nourishment from her placenta.

The giant anteater (*Myrmecophaga tridactyla*) eats mainly ants and termites. Instead of teeth it has a long, sticky tongue to scoop up prey. ▶

Food

Some mammals, such as hedgehogs, feed mainly on insects. They are known as insectivores. Others, such as sheep and horses, eat only plants. They are known as herbivores. Mammals that eat other animals are known as carnivores. Those that eat both plants and animals are called omnivores.

Insectivores

Insectivores are mostly small, nocturnal mammals, with a long snout for uncovering insects. Hedgehogs, shrews and moles are all insectivores. Most have lots of sharp teeth for biting through the outer casing of insects. Those that eat ants and termites, such as anteaters and pangolins, have a long, sticky tongue to trap their food. The giant anteater's tongue is about 60 cm long. Nearly all insectivores depend on smell to find their prey. They spend most of their waking hours hunting and eating.

Bats, such as this serotine bat (*Vespertilio serotinus*), find their prey by sending out high-pitched sounds that bounce back from objects, such as insects, in their path.

Herbivores

There are many types of herbivore. Some, such as deer, sheep and horses, eat mainly grasses. Others, such as squirrels and mice, eat mainly seeds, nuts and roots.

Rodents, such as squirrels and mice, have sharp incisor teeth at the front for gnawing hard roots, and flat molars at the back for grinding food. Sheep and horses, which graze on soft grasses, have no need for sharp incisor teeth. Their large molars and premolars grind up their food.

Like many herbivores, zebras have eyes on the sides of their heads for spotting predators as they eat.

Mammal teeth

Rodents have incisor teeth at the front for gnawing and molars at the back for chewing.

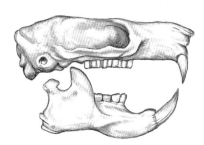

Herbivores that eat mainly soft grass have no incisors, just molars.

Carnivores have large canine teeth to rip into meat and sharp molars to tear it.

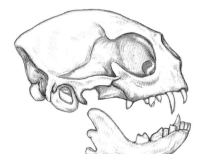

◄ Many herbivores, like this common dormouse (*Muscardinus avellanarius*), hibernate in winter when there is less plant food available.

Digestion

Herbivores have specially adapted digestive systems to cope with the cellulose in their diet. Cellulose is the material from which plants are made, and it takes a long time to break down.

Cows and sheep chew and swallow their food twice. At first the food goes to a special part of their stomach for several hours, where certain bacteria help to break it down. Then the food is brought back into their mouth, where it is chewed and swallowed again. This is called 'chewing the cud'.

Rabbits also eat their food twice. After a meal they pass soft droppings, but the droppings still contain nutrition. So the rabbits eat the droppings to get as much out of their food as possible.

Carnivores

Carnivores, such as dogs, cats and foxes, are all hunters of other animals for food. Most live on land, but some, such as otters and polar bears, spend much of their time in the water.

Carnivores' senses are well-suited for hunting, and most have excellent hearing, eyesight and smell for detecting prey. Their eyes are on the front of their head, which is good for judging distance. Carnivores have long, sharp canine teeth, sharp molars and strong jaw muscles for tearing into flesh and cutting through bones.

▲ A male and female lion (*Panthera leo*) watch their prey in Kenya.

Hunting

Many carnivores, such as the cheetah, are fast runners and rely on speed to catch their prey. The cheetah, which is the fastest of all cats, can reach speeds of 110 kilometres per hour.

Others, such as the lion, rely on stealth and surprise. They creep up on their prey with their bodies close to the ground before suddenly pouncing. Cheetahs, lions and other cats kill using their sharp claws to grip their victim before giving it a sharp bite to the neck.

Some carnivores, such as hyenas, are scavengers. They eat animals that they find dead, relying on other predators to do the killing. Spotted hyenas also hunt live prey, using a large pack of hyenas to bring down a wildebeest or zebra.

This spotted hyena (*Crocuta crocuta*) is eating a freshly killed wildebeest. ▼

WATER ANIMALS

Fish are not the only vertebrates that live in water. Water habitats provide food for many other animals.

▲ The otter (*Lutra lutra*) has dense, waterproof outer fur to keep it warm and dry.

The edible frog (*Rana esculenta*) swims with just its eyes above the water to hide from predators. ▼

Water life

Many frogs and toads spend much of their time in water. As young tadpoles, they live in the water like fish, with gills to breathe, and tails and fins to swim. As adults, they can swim well using their muscular back legs and webbed feet.

Whales and dolphins spend all their lives in water, but they must come to the surface to breathe air. Whales can swim underwater for up to 2 hours before taking a new breath because they breathe less frequently than other mammals. Dolphins are fast swimmers, helped by their streamlined bodies, powerful fins and paddle-like flippers.

Some birds, like this dipper (*Cinclus mexicanus*) dive underwater to find food on riverbeds. ▶

ANIMALS OF THE AIR

◀ The southern flying squirrel (*Glaucomys volans*) leaps from a tree.

Animals move through the air in two ways: by flying or by gliding. Flying animals flap their wings to push themselves forwards and upwards. Gliding animals use folds of skin to slow down the speed at which they fall.

Flying animals

Only birds and bats can fly. Birds' wings are covered with specially shaped feathers to lift them in the air. Bats have wings made from thin skin stretched over their front legs.

Both birds and bats have bones that are hollow and light, and both have powerful flight muscles.

Flying fish use their tail to propel themselves out of the water, and glide through the air beating their large fins. ▶

Gliding animals

Most gliding animals, such as tree frogs and flying squirrels, live in trees. Tree frogs use webbed toes to help slow them down as they leap from tree to tree. Flying squirrels have a fold of skin between their front and back legs which they stretch out and use as a parachute.

LAND ANIMALS

Most land vertebrates have four legs to support their weight.

▲ The capuchin monkey (*Cabus albifrons*) uses its long tail as well as its legs to climb trees.

Some animals, such as deer and cattle, spend most of their time balancing on all four legs. Others, such as rabbits and squirrels, can sit up on their haunches so they can look around from a better height. Humans, and flightless birds, such as penguins and ostriches, walk on two legs. Most other land vertebrates use four legs to walk and run.

Burrowing animals, such as moles and badgers, have streamlined bodies that move easily through tunnels, and spade-shaped front feet for digging. Animals that jump, such as kangaroos and frogs, have long, muscular hind legs.

Animals that live in trees are specially adapted for climbing. They are light in weight and are able to hold on to branches in a particular way. Squirrels run along branches by gripping the bark with their claws. Geckos have special pads on their toes that stick to vertical surfaces. Monkeys clasp branches with their fingers and toes, and many have a long tail to help them keep their balance.

The European mole (*Talpa europaea*) is blind. It uses smell to detect prey. ▼

HOT AND COLD CLIMATES

All animals need to be able to alter their body temperature so they do not get too hot or too cold. They also need water to survive. In the hot desert and the cold polar regions, animals have become specially adapted to cope with the conditions there.

▲ Camels can survive for months without drinking water by getting moisture from the plants that they eat.

Deserts

Reptiles in the desert use the sun to heat up and move into the shade to cool down. Many desert animals have large ears that help lose heat. At night, some animals burrow into the ground for warmth. Many desert animals obtain most of the water they need from the food that they eat, since there is little water in the desert.

Polar regions

Animals that live in the polar regions need extra help to keep them warm. Seals and whales have a thick layer of blubber under their skin. Polar bears have both fat and a thick fur coat.

Small mammals, such as lemmings, burrow underground during the winter to keep warm. Some animals, such as icefish, have a natural antifreeze in their blood which means they can survive in sub-zero temperatures.

Emperor penguins (*Aptenodytes forsteri*) have dense, waterproof feathers and thick layers of fat under their skin to help them survive the Antarctic temperatures. ▼

THE FUTURE FOR ANIMALS

Scientists are discovering new species of animals all the time, but many species are disappearing as a result of human action. As more cities are built and land is cleared for farming or logging, the habitats of many species are destroyed.

Threats

People have hunted many species, such as the rhino, to near extinction. Rhinos and elephants are still being illegally hunted for their tusks. While conservation groups and governments do their best to protect species, many are still under threat.

Pollution from industry and farming pours into the world's rivers and lakes, killing fish and animals that live in the water. Oil spills from giant tankers can wreck a coastal habitat which takes years to recover.

The horn of this black rhino (*Rhinoceros bicornis*) has been illegally removed by poachers. ▶

Genetic engineering

For hundreds of years, animals have been specially bred for certain features, such as high milk production. More recently, scientists have been using a technique called genetic engineering, which alters the genetic material of a living thing to change its characteristics. Genetic engineering can be used to create a leaner, faster-growing pig, or a hen that produces more eggs.

▲ These conservationists are attaching a radio collar to a tiger (*Panthera tigris*) so they can follow its movements and learn more about its needs.

Some people are worried that genetic engineering might accidentally produce harmful bacteria or viruses, or that it might damage the environment. Others do not think we should be changing the genetic makeup of living creatures for moral reasons. Most people agree that we need to think carefully about our impact on other animal species for our own benefit as well as the whole animal kingdom.

◄ Chimpanzees (*Pan troglodytes*) share more characteristics with human beings than any other animal.

GLOSSARY

ambush To attack an enemy by surprise from a hiding place.

antifreeze A substance within a liquid that lowers the temperature at which it freezes.

barbel A long, thin growth that projects from the mouths or nostrils of some fish.

camouflage The way that animals hide by blending in with their surroundings.

canine A pointed tooth that pierces through flesh.

carnivores Animals that feed mainly on meat.

cellulose The substance from which plants are made, which forms the walls of plant cells.

cold-blooded Animals whose body temperature is similar to their surroundings.

conservation Protecting something from loss or harm.

embryos The early stages of an animal before birth or hatching.

evolved Developed gradually over a long time.

extinction Destroyed or wiped out.

fertilisation The process in which a male and a female reproductive cell join and form a new cell.

fry Young fish.

genetic engineering The scientific altering of genes or genetic material to change the characteristics of living things.

habitat The type of area where an animal or plant naturally lives.

herbivores Animals that eat only plant food.

hibernate To enter a deep sleep that lasts most of the winter.

incisor A chisel-shaped tooth with a cutting edge.

incubate To hatch eggs by sitting on them to keep them warm.

insectivores Animals that eat mainly insects.

larvae Young animals, such as tadpoles, that develop into adults by a complete change in body shape.

metamorphosis A major change in an animal's body shape during its life cycle.

molars Teeth with a broad surface for grinding food.

nectar A sweet liquid produced by flowers to attract insects and birds that carry out pollination.

nocturnal An animal that sleeps during the day and is active at night.

omnivores Animals that eat both plant and animal food.

parasites Animals or plants that live on or inside the body of another species from which they get their food.

placenta An organ in mammals that passes nutrition between the unborn young and its mother.

polar regions The regions around the North or South Pole.

predator A hunting animal that kills and eats other animals.

prey An animal that is killed and eaten by other animals.

scavengers Animals that feed on the remains of dead animals or plants.

streamlined Shaped to move easily through air or water.

territories Areas that animals defend against others of the same species.

vegetation Plant life.

vertebrates Animals with a backbone.

warm-blooded Animals whose blood stays about the same temperature, regardless of the air or water around them. Warm-blooded animals control their body temperature by burning food.

FINDING OUT MORE

100 Things You Should Know About pack: *Insects & Spiders/Reptiles & Amphibians/Birds/Mammals* (Raintree, 2002)

Animal Young: Amphibians/Fish/Birds/Insects/Reptiles/Mammals by Rod Theodorou (Heinemann, 1999)

Classifying Living Things: Classifying: Amphibians/Fish/Birds/Insects/Reptiles/Mammals by Andrew Solway (Heinemann, 2003)

DK Animal Encyclopedia (Dorling Kindersley, 2000)

From Egg to Adult series: The Life Cycle of Reptiles/Mammals/Fish/Birds/Amphibians/Insects (Heinemann, 2003)

Illustrated Encyclopedia of Animals by Fran Pickering (Chrysalis, 2003)

Junior Nature Guides: Birds/Butterflies/Insects/Mammals/Sealife (Chrysalis, 2003)

Life Cycles: Cats and Other Mammals/Butterflies and Other Insects/Ducks and Other Birds/Frogs and Other Amphibians by Sally Morgan (Chrysalis, 2001)

Living Nature: Amphibians/Fish/Birds/Insects/Reptiles/Mammals by Angela Royston (Chrysalis, 2002)

Living Things: Adaptation/Classification/Survival and Change/Food Chains and Webs/Life Cycles/Cells and Systems by Anita Ganeri (Heinemann, 2001)

The Wayland Book of Common British Mammals by Shirley Thompson (Hodder Wayland, 2000)

What's the Difference?: Amphibians/Fish/Birds/Insects/Reptiles/Mammals by Stephen Savage (Hodder Wayland, 2002)

Picture acknowledgements

Cover: Corbis (Kevin Schafer).
Inside: Bruce Coleman 6 (Franco Banfi), 6–7 (Andrew J Purcell), 8 (Hans Reinhard), 9 (Kim Taylor), 11 (Mark Carwardine), 14–15 (Jane Burton), 15 (Jane Burton), 16 (M P L Fogden), 17 (John Cancalosi), 19 (Gerald Cubitt), 21 (Fred Bruemmer), 22 (Bruce Coleman Inc), 23 (Kim Taylor), 24 (Jane Burton), 26 (HPH Photography), 27 (Brian J Coates), 28 (Francisco Futil), 29 top (Ken Balcomb), 30 (Luiz Claudio Marigo), 31 (Kim Taylor), 32 (Luiz Claudio Marigo), 33 (George McCarthy), 35 (Peter Davey), 36 top (Paul Van Gaalen), 36 bottom (Ingo Arndt), 37 (Dieter & Mary Plage), 38 (Kim Taylor), 40 (Luiz Claudio Marigo), 41 (Andrew Purcell), 43 (Hans Reinhard), 44 (Peter Davey), 45 top (Michael P Price). Natural History Photo Library 12 (Daniel Heuclin), 34 (Martin Harvey), 39 (Norbert Wu). Oxford Scientific Films 4–5 (Martyn Colbeck), 29 bottom (Alan Root/Okapia). Tony Stone *title page* (Art Wolfe), 20 (Ron Dahlquist), 45 bottom (Tim Davis). Wayland Picture Library 2, 42.
Artwork: pages 5 and 23 by Simon Borrough; pages 10, 13, 18 and 25 by Peter Bull Art Studio.

INDEX